Getting Around Through the Years

How Transportation
Has Changed in
Living Memory

Clare Lewis

Heinemann
raintree

© 2015 Heinemann Raintree
an imprint of Capstone Global Library, LLC
Chicago, Illinois

To contact Capstone Global Library please
call 800-747-4992, or visit our web site
www.capstonepub.com

Edited by Clare Lewis and Holly Beaumont
Designed by Philippa Jenkins
Picture research by Tracy Cummins
Production by Victoria Fitzgerald
Originated by Capstone Global Library Ltd
Printed and bound in China by Leo Paper Group

18 17 16 15 14
10 9 8 7 6 5 4 3 2 1

Library of Congress Cataloging-in-Publication Data
Lewis, Clare, 1976-
  Getting around through the years : how transportation has changed in living memory / Clare Lewis.
    pages cm.—(History in living memory)
  Includes bibliographical references and index.
  ISBN 978-1-4846-0924-8 (hb)—ISBN 978-1-4846-0929-3 (pb)—ISBN 978-1-4846-0939-2 (ebook) 1. Transportation—History..
I. Title.

HE151.L457 2015
388—dc23   2014015028

This book has been officially leveled by using the F&P Text Level Gradient™ Leveling System.

Acknowledgments
We would like to thank the following for permission to reproduce photographs: Capstone Press: Philippa Jenkins, 1 Right, 1 Top Left; Corel: Reuben T. Parsons, 4; Getty Images: AFP PHOTO/JIJI PRESS, 12, Alexis DUCLOS/Gamma-Rapho, 16, Car Culture ® Collection, 19, Dennis Oulds/Central Press, 14, Fox Photos, 15, Lambert, 10, The AGE/Fairfax Media, 8, The Denver Post, 7; Glow Images: Superstock, 11; Shutterstock: Everett Collection, 5, Flas100, Design Element, Hung Chung Chih, 17, Back Cover, i4lcocl2, 23 Bottom, kaczor58, 23 Middle, Maksim Toome, 22 Top Right, Monkey Business Images, 20, Olegusk, 23 Top, Pavel L Photo and Video, 21, Pressmaster, Cover Bottom, Rob Wilson, 22 Top Left, Studio DMM Photography, Designs & Art, Design Element; SuperStock: Marka, Cover Top, The Francis Frith Collection, 6, 9; Thinkstock: Anton Sokolov, 22 Bottom, Comstock, 18; Wikimedia: NASA, 13.

Every effort has been made to contact copyright holders of material reproduced in this book. Any omissions will be rectified in subsequent printings if notice is given to the publisher.

Some words are shown in bold, **like this**. You can find them in the glossary on page 23.

Contents

What Is History in Living Memory?

Some history happened a very long time ago. Nobody alive now lived through it.

Some history did not happen very long ago. Our parents, grandparents, and adult friends can tell us how life used to be. We call this history in living memory.

How Has Getting Around Changed in Living Memory?

Transportation has changed a lot since your grandparents were young. There were fewer cars then, so the roads were quieter.

More people walked or rode bikes
to get around. Journeys often took
longer than they do today.

How Did People in the 1950s Make Long Journeys?

In the 1950s, traveling by airplane was very expensive. To visit other countries, people often traveled by ship.

Buses and trains were used more for long journeys. Some people went on vacation by **steam train**.

What Were Cars Like in the 1950s?

Cars became more popular in the 1950s. People didn't have to wear seat belts or use car seats for children back then. Lots of children could squeeze in the backseat!

When your parents and grandparents were young, there was no **GPS** in cars. If they got lost, they had to read a paper map to find their way.

What Changes Took Place in the 1960s?

In 1969, a new airplane called Concorde took its first flight. It could fly faster than the speed of sound.

The first astronauts traveled by space rocket in the 1960s. Neil Armstrong was the first person to walk on the Moon.

When Did Flying Become More Popular?

In the 1970s, the first jumbo jets began to fly in the skies. They could carry 300 people at a time.

Flying became cheaper and easier for people. Families began traveling more often to other countries for vacations.

What Were Trains Like in the 1980s?

More people had cars in the 1980s, but trains were still popular. In the 1980s, high-speed railroads were developed. They ran using electricity.

They could take people on long journeys very quickly. Some trains today are even faster.

Does Transportation Cause Problems?

In the 1990s, people became worried about so many cars on the roads. Diesel and gasoline cause **pollution**. This is harmful to us and to the planet.

Hybrid cars were invented, which could run using electricity and gasoline. Engineers are still trying to find ways to power cars that won't harm the environment.

How Do You Travel Today?

So many people travel by car now that traffic jams can be a problem. Some people like to walk or ride bikes, just as people did in the past.

Many people still travel by train, but now **steam trains** are just for fun. Airplanes can transport people quickly, but some people still like to travel by ship.

Picture Quiz

Which of these cars is from the 1950s?

A

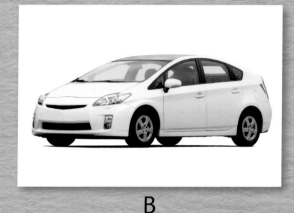

B

C

How can you tell?

Picture Glossary

pollution
harmful gases in the air

GPS (Global Positioning System)
electronic system in a car that tells you how to get to places

steam train
train that is powered using fire, which heats water to make steam

Find Out More

Books

Hunter, Nick. *Talking About the Past* (History at Home). Chicago: Heinemann Library, 2014.

Rissman, Rebecca. *Taking a Trip* (Comparing Past and Present). Chicago: Heinemann Library, 2014.

Web site

FactHound offers a safe, fun way to find Internet sites related to this book. All of the sites on FactHound have been researched by our staff.

Here's all you do: Visit www.facthound.com
Type in this code: 9781484609248

Index